William S

King Lear Companion

Includes Study Guide, Historical Context, Biography, and Character Index

BookCaps™ Study Guides

www.bookcaps.com

Table of Contents

Historical Context

King Lear was first performed for King James I of Britain in December of 1606 although Shakespearean scholars believe it was written a year earlier, in 1605. It is possible that William Shakespeare wrote the play about the same time he wrote *Othello* (there are similar plot points) and as *Measure for Measure*, where they are similarities in language.

The story of King Lear originated in the tale of an early Celtic king in the land of what would one day be England. Many stories of ancient kings were recorded in *The Chronicles of England, Scotland, and Ireland* by Ralph Holinshed (first published in 1577) and Shakespeare used some elements of the tale of King Leir (sic) to construct his play, although he also borrowed snippets here and there from other stories and myths. He was apparently inspired by an earlier play called *King Leir*, but changed most of the story line and characters. He also used a contemporary poem for inspiration and a work of fiction, *Arcadia*, by Sir Philip Sidney. One of his inspirations may have been an anti-Jesuit attack that appeared in 1602, written by Samuel Harsnett, in which demonic allies of the Jesuits are mentioned. In King Lear, one of his characters, Tom of Bedlam, mentions the demons in his ravings. During the early 1600's, under the reign of the Stuart dynasty, there was much anti-Catholic sentiment while Britain went through its transition years from a Catholic nation to a Protestant one.

Shakespeare's version of King Lear's story is the one that is best known today. It was written in the last period of the playwright's productivity – he has forty-one recognized plays and *King Lear* was his twenty-ninth work.

William Shakespeare was a popular playwright during his lifetime and King Lear was a popular play, going through two editions fairly quickly, being first published in quarto form and then in the "complete" works put together in 1663 by Shakespeare's colleagues after his death. The latter is known as the "First Folio".

Shakespeare was born in 1564 in the rural county of Warwickshire, the son of John Shakespeare and Mary Arden of Stratford-upon-Avon. The Shakespeares were middle class; John made gloves for a living and did well enough to sit as a councillor and send his son to a local fee-paying school. Mary Arden came from a slightly better social background than her husband; the Ardens were land owners.

William was not to receive a university education, as the family had fallen on financial hardship during his teens. Later critics wonder at how a man without a university degree could write so well, but Shakespeare's talents lie not only in his writing ability but in his astute assessment of human nature and human relationships.

Shakespeare married young, after the older woman he was seeing became pregnant. He became a father to a daughter, Susanna, when he had barely turned nineteen, and two years later Anne, his wife, gave birth to twins, a son and a daughter. The three children were the only children that Shakespeare is known to have fathered, and none of them left descendants.

While still in his early twenties Shakespeare went to London – his reasons are unclear, but it is obvious he was keen to pursue a career in the theatre. He joined a company of actors and eventually turned to writing, where his genius shone. King Lear would become just one play out of an amazing body of work the playwright would leave to the world after his death in 1626.

Plot Overview

Shakespeare's King Lear was based on a mythical story of an ancient king of pre-Christian Britain. The story likely had elements of truth to it, but Shakespeare presented it in a more contemporary format that his audiences could understand.

King Lear, an aged monarch, has decided to divide his kingdom up among his three daughters Goneril, Regan, and Cordelia. Goneril is married to the Duke of Albany and Regan to the Duke of Cornwall. Cordelia is still single, and two men are residing in court, competing for her hand in marriage (and her dowry) – the King of France and the Duke of Burgundy.   *3 daughters*

When Lear calls his servants, retainers, court and family together he is pleased with the obsequious flattery he receives at the hand of his two older daughters, Goneril and Regan. He does not realize that they are probably already scheming to take away all of his power. Lear has decided to give control over to his daughters and their husbands but not to relinquish quite everything – he fully expects to retain some influence at court and be given the respect due a monarch of his age and experience.

Lear's third daughter, his favorite, Cordelia, refuses to use false flattery with her father and he is outraged and decides to cut her dowry down to a miniscule size. The King of France, smitten by Cordelia, wishes to marry her regardless, and they are sent from the kingdom back to France.

In a subplot that mirrors the main story, one of Lear's supporters, the Earl of Gloucester is soon betrayed by his illegitimate son Edmund – who tells him his legitimate son Edgar is plotting against it. Goneril and Regan have already turned against their father with the avid support of Regan's husband the Duke of Cornwall. They alienate the Earl of Kent, who is sent away by Lear, believing him to be unfaithful to his King. In time, Gloucester is blinded by the Duke of Cornwall and is helped by his son Edgar, now banished and disguised as a peasant.

One stormy night, after being bitterly disappointed by his second daughter, Regan, Lear blunders out into the night, ranting that he cannot take such treatment any longer. His Fool, formerly a servant of Cordelia's, goes with him, and protects the King, who is clearly becoming unhinged. Eventually, they hide in a shelter with Edgar, who is posing as a peasant named Tom.

In time, the news comes that the King of France has landed, coming to the aid of Lear. However, Edmund has managed to find enough troops to support his cause, and attacks the French at Dover. Cordelia is in the camp there, and is reunited with her father, and their differences resolved. Edmund takes Cordelia and Lear prisoner, and Gloucester and Edgar are also at Dover, and Gloucester dies, but not before Edgar reveals his true identity. Edmund defeats the French and orders Cordelia to be hanged, which brings on Lear's sudden death. Meanwhile, Goneril has killed Regan and then herself as a result of their rivalry over Edmund.

Edgar kills Edmund and now that all the protagonists are gone, it is left up to him, and the Earl of Kent to restore the kingdom.

Themes

Appearance

The appearance of what something is plays a large part in the development of the plot of *King Lear*. Goneril and Regan use flattery to win their father's love and Edmund pretends to be loyal to his father while secretly plotting behind his back against his half-brother Edgar. Oswald appears to be steadfast and loyal, but, in fact, it is Kent who is loyal. The tragedy of Lear's poor judgment leads to violent death, suicide, and the blinding of Gloucester.

Betrayal

The theme of betrayal runs through the play as the daughters turn against their father, and Edmund against Gloucester. Lear voices his deep hurt when he says "How sharper than a serpent's tooth is it to have a thankless child!" for he feels he gave so much to his daughters, and they have little regard for him or his feelings. Gloucester too is betrayed and loses his sight, thanks for the selfish ambition of the illegitimate son he raised in his household.

Disguise

The use of disguise is central to the plot of King Lear. Two important characters, the Earl of Kent who is banished from Lear's court when he interferes with the King's plan to disinherit Cordelia and Edgar who is banished when his father Gloucester thinks he is plotting to overthrow him both take on a disguise. Their roles move the story along, and Shakespeare makes an intriguing point that the good must hide themselves in order to usurp the bad.

The Elements

The weather and particularly stormy weather is a motif that occurs at an important point of the play – Lear, Gloucester, and Edgar spend time wandering around the heath and encounter weather that parallels the storms going on in their lives. The upheaval of betrayal for these men and the unsettled times in Lear's kingdom mirror the tempestuous weather on the heath. These men must "weather the storm" before peace can be restored again.

Nature

Many scenes in *King Lear* take place out of doors, with a symbolic return of man to nature. Lear, Gloucester, Kent, and Edgar all take cover in a rustic shelter to get out of the storm, representing nature's wrath. Later Edgar takes his blinded father Gloucester to Dover, and a pivotal scene takes place in a field not far from the cliffs. The antagonists' parts in the play tend to be staged indoors, perhaps as a nod to man's "civilized" state not being so civilized at all and the character of man has become something less living in an unnatural state.

Family Relationships

The plot of *King Lear* is centered on family relationships and the contrasts between their elements of goodness and destruction are clearly shown. While Goneril and Regan despise their father and treat him disrespectfully, his third daughter Cordelia is devoted to him in her own quiet way; Gloucester turns on his son Edgar when his second son Edmund reveals Edgar's supposed treachery and it is Edgar's devoted care that saves the blinded Earl in the end.

Madness

The madness of Lear is central to the plot of the play, and his wilful misunderstanding of Cordelia's nature may be the sign of incipient mental illness. His giving Goneril and Regan so much power may be a hint of disintegration as well, as he surely knew the nature of his three daughters to predict what could happen. Lear's madness is paralleled in the mock-madness of Edgar, who as Poor Tom, takes on a persona in order to disguise his true origins. In Lear's case, the madness is real.

Power

The holding of power and the quest for more is another prominent theme of *King Lear*. Lear has held sway in his kingdom for many years but decides it is time for a change – it is he who directs how this should go, and makes some bad decisions, much as those in power often do. The quest for power drives the action forward in the case of Goneril, Regan, Albany, and Edmund and ultimately leads to their downfall. The theme of power is used to contrast those who seek it and those who don't and obviously divides the two sides in the conflict.

Blindness

Shakespeare has the characters speak about blindness several times in the play in a metaphorical sense. King Lear is blinded by his emotions when he cannot or will not see that his older daughters are devious plotters and his youngest an honest loving child. The Earl of Gloucester is literally blinded in a fight with Albany and spends the rest of the play being led by a young man he does not realize is his son. Both Lear and Gloucester represent those who are blind to the truth and the misery that can come of this.

Love and Loyalty

Although not a tale of romantic love, King Lear does portray love of different kinds: familial love and loyalty (Cordelia for Lear, Edgar for Gloucester) and personal love and loyalty (Kent for Lear, the Servants for Gloucester). Love and loyalty reflect the goodness in human nature, and their opposites are found in Goneril, Regan, Albany, and Edmund whose goals are purely self-interested. In the end love and loyalty triumph although at a terrible cost.

Character Summaries

King Lear

King Lear is based upon a mythical character who may have been an early monarch of Britain in pre-Christian time. The myth was still commonly known in England during Shakespeare's lifetime. In Shakespeare's play, the King is old (in his eighties) and has decided to divide his kingdom among his three daughters. He becomes angry with his youngest daughter so divides it between the two older daughters, Goneril and Regan. This in time leads to his downfall and his tragic death.

Goneril

Goneril is the eldest of King Lear's three daughters and the wife of the Duke of Albany. After flattering her father and conniving to convince him to give up his kingdom in all but name, Goneril turns against her father once she has her portion and begins treat him poorly and in time, to plot his demise. Her husband turns against her before the end of the play as she falls in love with Edmund, the son of the Earl of Gloucester.

Regan

Regan is the second and middle daughter of King Lear and is much like her sister Goneril. She plays up to and flatters her father who believes she and Goneril truly love him. After she receives her portion of her father's kingdom, she also turns against him and feels little compassion for his miserable state. Regan is married to the Duke of Cornwall, a nasty and vindictive man. Regan dies by poison at the end of the play at the hands of her sister Goneril, who then kills herself.

Cordelia

Cordelia is the youngest of the three daughters of King Lear. At the beginning of the play, she is being courted by the King of France and the Duke of Burgundy. She decides to marry the King of France. When Lear is dividing up his kingdom in the first scene of Act 1, Cordelia refuses to flatter him, but behaves as she has always done. Lear banishes her and leaves her no land. In the end, Cordelia is reunited with her father shortly before he dies.

Duke of Albany

The Duke of Albany is married to Goneril, King Lear's oldest daughter. As a man in that time period, he has as much, if not more, influence in their portion of the kingdom as his wife does. Albany is torn between supporting his wife and supporting her father, but his sense of ethics and strong character win out in the end as he turns against Goneril and supports Lear.

Duke of Cornwall

He is married to Regan, Lear's middle daughter. As a man in that time period, he has as much, if not more, influence in their portion of the kingdom as his wife does. Unlike his brother-in-law Albany, Cornwall joins in his wife's scheming against her father to usurp his power. He also allies himself with Edmund, son of Gloucester. In the end, he loses his life due to his scheming.

Earl of Gloucester

The Earl fights against the corruption of the daughters of his King but never gives up his loyalty to Lear, even after losing his sight in an assault by the Duke of Cornwall. A subplot of the play, Gloucester's divided loyalties of his sons Edmund and Edgar, mirror the machinations of Lear's daughters against him. He goes to Dover with his "good" son, disguised as a peasant, to lend support to his king.

Earl of Kent

A faithful supporter of the King, Kent gets wind that treachery is in the air, and is placed in the stocks for hitting Goneril's servant. Lear banishes him but Kent stays in the area, taking on a disguise and getting himself hired as a servant to the King. Throughout the play, he serves as Lear's faithful servant and intervenes on the old King's behalf when necessary. At the end, he expresses his feelings about his demise – the King is dead and he will soon die too as his work on Earth is done.

Edgar

Edgar is the legitimate son of the King of Gloucester and is slightly older than his half-brother Edmund. Edmund tricks their father into thinking Edgar is plotting against him (the Earl) and Gloucester banishes Edgar. Edgar lives rough and when his shelter is found by the King, Kent, and the Fool, pretends to be a peasant ("Poor Tom") who is out of his mind. In time, he rescues his father who has been blinded.

Edmund

Edmund is the illegitimate son of the Earl of Gloucester, the result of a brief romance. Gloucester maintains he treats him no differently than his son Edgar, who is legitimate. Edmund begrudges his brother his inheritance (he is not due anything because he is illegitimate) and swears he will get rid of Edgar so he may take what is "rightfully" his, as he feels he is the better man. Edmund sides with Goneril and Regan and leads them both on, and his having an actual affair with Goneril is almost certain.

Oswald

Goneril's faithful steward, Oswald plots against her father for their King's downfall. He serves as a go-between and a spy. Oswald is seen as a weak person without ethics, one who would sell anyone down the river to better his own position. This is the Earl of Kent's opinion of Oswald and Kent finds himself banished when he expresses what he thinks. Oswald is the perfect obsequious servant and dies for his mistress, Goneril.

Fool

The King's Fool, who was originally Cordelia's before she went to France, takes over her role as Lear's protector. He spends much of his time in the play spouting nonsense doggerel and silly rhymes – disguised as pithy observations of what is going on around him. The Fool accompanies Lear when he leaves the castle and wanders around the heath and makes sure he comes to no harm.

King of France

Early in the play Lear mentions the King of France as a possible husband for Cordelia and, in fact, he is staying with the court while he competes with another suitor. Although Lear cuts Cordelia's dowry down to a minimum, France still wants to marry her, for he has grown to love her. Later he invades Lear's kingdom when it is threatened by those who have turned against the King.

Duke of Burgundy

The Duke of Burgundy is competing for Cordelia's hand with the King of France. He has no interest in her once Lear decides his youngest daughter will be cut out of her share of his land and holdings. He serves as a contrast to the King of France, who loves Cordelia despite her lack of dowry.

Servants

Various servants and other retainers appear in the play. In one pivotal scene, after Cornwall blinds Gloucester, the Duke of Albany's servants leave in disgust, deserting their master for such heinous actions against an innocent man.

Scene Summaries

Act One

Act 1, Scene 1

The play opens at King Lear's palace, where three men, the Earl of Kent, the Earl of Gloucester, and Edmund (Gloucester's illegitimate son) are discussing court matters. Kent is saying how he believes the king favors the Duke of Albany over the Duke of Cornwall. Gloucester remarks that since the kingdom is going to be divided up it is hard to tell which man the king favors.

Kent changes the subject and asks Gloucester, gesturing at Edmund, if the young man is his son. Gloucester admits that he is, even though he is often embarrassed to admit it. Kent asks him why, and Gloucester replies that Edmund's mother has a faulty character for bearing an illegitimate son and, therefore, the boy is tainted, as well. He defends himself by saying he has a legitimate son only slightly older, but he, Gloucester, does not favor that son. Gloucester won't disown Edmund, because, as he says, his mother was beautiful and they had a good time conceiving him. Gloucester formally introduces Edmund to Kent, explaining that the latter has been abroad for nine years in the army.

King Lear enters, following a servant carrying a coronet. Behind the King are the Dukes of Albany with his wife Goneril and the Duke of Cornwall with his wife Regan. Goneril and Regan are the daughters of Lear. Also with them is Cordelia, his youngest daughter. They are accompanied by other members of the court.

Lear orders Gloucester to fetch the Lords of France and Burgundy and the Earl leaves.

Lear takes a map from a servant and begins to address the court. tells him he is approaching old age and wants to divide his kingdo. He says he is publicly declaring his daughters' dowries and that his youngest unmarried daughter's hand is marriage is being sought by the Kings of France and the Duke of Burgundy, who have been residing at court while they compete for her hand.

Lear addresses his daughters and asks which one loves him the most, for she will get the lion share of his holdings. He turns to Goneril, his oldest daughter, first. Goneril speaks gushingly of how much she loves her father – that no one could love him more, that words cannot express her adoration. Her sister Cordelia says under her breath that she herself will speak simply of her love, without all the exaggeration.

Lear indicates on the map the area of his land that will go to Goneril and her husband Albany. Then he asks Regan to speak. Regan tells him that her love for her father is as deep as Goneril's but that her sister has not expressed it as strongly as she herself, Regan, feels it. Cordelia again quietly says, almost to herself, that how can she better her sisters' declarations but that she does know her love is stronger than can be put into words. Her father responds by saying she will be given as good a section of the kingdom as Goneril received.

Lear then asks Cordelia what she has to say. She replies "nothing". Her father urges her to say more, to express her feelings for him. Finally, Cordelia tells him that she loves him so much she will only be able to love her future husband half as much. The king finds her response not emotional enough, and Cordelia protests that she is only being truthful. Lear sputters that he is cutting her out of the family inheritance, although she is the one he has loved the most.

' goes to her sisters, and the king says he will live
er daughters, first with one and then the other. His
run the kingdom, while Lear retains the title and the
ngs.

Kent tries to advise Lear not to be foolish, not to offer his coronet to
his sons-in-law. He tells the king that Cordelia does not love him
least just because her speech was not an exercise in flattery. Lear
tells him to be quiet, or fear for his life. Kent scoffs at this. They
exchange heated remarks and Lear draws his sword. His sons-in-law
beg him to calm down.

Lear gives Kent six days to get out of his kingdom, or to be put to
death. Kent agrees to go, encouraging Cordelia and disparaging
Goneril and Regan for their false flattery. He leaves and the King of
France and Duke of Burgundy enter. Lear tells the two that the price
for Cordelia has fallen; she is now unloved and unwanted by her
own father.   The King of France confesses he is confused by Lear's
change of heart.

Cordelia speaks up and begs him to reconsider what she said, what
her true feelings are, that she does not speak with empty flattery.
Lear is unbending and tells the Duke of Burgundy there is no dowry.
The Duke rejects Cordelia, who is relieved. The King of France,
smitten with Cordelia for her own sake, says he will take her as his
wife. Lear happily gives her away and leaves with his entourage.

Cordelia calls after her sisters as they leave, calling them false, and
saying their father would be better cared for by her. Regan and
Goneril tell her she better make the most of things with the King of
France, who has rescued her from a cheerless life.

Cordelia leaves with France and her sisters talk about their father, saying he is fickle in his old age, cranky and lacking self-control. They plan to keep a watchful eye on him, knowing his capricious behavior could spell trouble for them.

Act 1, Scene 2

The scene opens at the Earl of Gloucester's palace. His son Edmund enters with a letter. He is complaining to himself about his status as a bastard, feeling that is unfair. He does not understand why he is considered inferior just because his parents were never married. Edmund is convinced that children born of passion are stronger than children born to the married, whose passion has died. He addresses his absent half-brother Edgar and says he will have his inheritance. He waves the letter and says his victory lies in the message in his hand.

His father Gloucester appears, talking to himself. He is muttering about how Kent has been banished and that France has left with Cordelia, very unhappy with Lear who has relinquished much of his power on what seems like a whim. Suddenly he notices Edmund and asks him if there is any news.

Edmund makes a show of hiding his letter, saying he has no news. His father asks him what it is that he's been reading. The older man insists on seeing it, wondering why Edmund would make such an effort to hide "nothing".

Edmund makes excuses, saying it is from his brother and their father should not see it. Finally, Gloucester grabs it and reads it aloud. It sounds like a letter of conspiracy, Edgar asking Edmund to help him usurp their father. Edmund tells Gloucester the letter was thrown through his window; he claims the handwriting is that of his brother. His father demands to know if this is an ongoing thing, this discontent of Edgar's. Edmund says it is not, but he has heard Edgar say that aged fathers should give up their power to their grown sons.

Gloucester is livid; he wants to have Edgar arrested. Edmund advises his father to take it slowly, or he might ruin his own reputation. He maintains that Edgar is merely testing Edmund's loyalty, which Gloucester should not doubt, and he offers to find Edgar. Gloucester becomes maudlin, blaming the eclipses of the sun and moon for ruining relationships, pitting son against father. He asks Edmund to sound Edgar out, but to do it carefully and with subtlety.

Gloucester leaves. Edmund talks about how stupid his father is – blaming things on the moon, sun and stars. Edmund himself does not believe that the stars have any influence over man.

Edgar enters. Edmund puts on a solemn face and speaks of ominous eclipses in a serious tone. Edgar greets him and asks him what is wrong. Edmund begins to talk about the dire influence of astrology, much to Edgar's puzzlement. Edmund asks his brother if he had seen their father lately and what his mood had been – Edgar replies that it was the night before, and his father was the same as ever. Edmund tells him their father is in a foul mood, and his anger is directed at Edgar. He advises Edgar to hide in his brother's room and stay out of Gloucester's way and to arm himself if he goes out alone. Edgar takes Edmund's bedroom key and leaves.

Edmund laughs to himself, at his father and brother's gullibility. He brags that he will win his rightful inheritance by his wits.

Act 1, Scene 3

The scene begins at the Duke of Albany's palace. Goneril enters with her steward Oswald. She asks her steward if her father had struck her officer because he told off his Fool. The steward replies in the affirmative.

Goneril comments on how out of control her father is and how he is upsetting the entire household. He is becoming difficult to live with. She tells Oswald that she does not want to see her father when he returns from hunting, that he is to tell Lear that she is sick.

Hunting horns are heard; Lear is returning. Goneril tells Oswald to make sure her father knows she is upset with him. She says if he doesn't like it, he can go stay with Regan. She calls him an "old fool" who acts like a baby, and like a child must be scolded when he steps out of line. She instructs Oswald to spread the word among the staff and servants about her father's unacceptable behavior.

Act One, Scene 4

Kent enters a room in the palace, in disguise. He is talking to himself, saying he hopes he can disguise his voice, as well. His purpose is to get back into his king's good graces without Lear catching on to his true identity. He hears the hunting horns announcing the return of his king.

Lear enters and asks Kent who he is. He responds that he is a man; Lear wants to know what his business is, and what he does. Kent says he is but a loyal servant to whomever he serves, a poor man who is seeking a job with Lear.

Lear asks if he if knows who he is, and Kent replies that he does not, but that there is something about the king that makes him want to work for him, that Lear has an air of authority.

Kent lists his own virtues, his greatest being able to keep a secret and strong determination. He can also ride and run and deliver a straightforward message. Lear wants to know how old he is and Kent admits to being forty-eight. Lear says he will take him on as his servant, and if he still likes him by the time dinner is done, Kent can stay on permanently.

Lear sends a servant to fetch his Fool. Oswald enters, and Lear asks him where his daughter is. Oswald brushes by him, almost snubbing the king. Lear is astonished and sends a knight to bring Oswald back. The knight returns without Oswald and Lear demands to know where "that mongrel" is, and the knight says he rudely refused to come with him. The knight comments that Lear is not being treated with respect. Lear agrees with him, saying he had thought it was his imagination.

Lear again demands to know where his fool is. The knight says he has been pining for Cordelia, who has left for France.

Oswald returns and Lear curses at him, calling him names and hitting him. Kent, now Lear's loyal servant, trips Oswald and earns Lear's respect. The king gives him some money.

Lear's Fool finally shows up and gives his silly hat to Kent which he says is a reward for siding with Lear, who is out of favor. He tells Kent that Lear has alienated two daughters and exiled a third, although she is better off for it.

The Fool recites a couple of verses, meant as advice to Lear, but the king shrugs them off as being "nothing". The Fool chides Lear for cutting his crown in two and giving half to each of his older daughters. He jokes that Lear has made his daughters his mother, and they now have control of him. Lear threatens to have the Fool whipped, and he replies that he is whipped when he is right and when he is wrong, and when he is neither.

Goneril enters and tells her father his followers are rioting. He questions half-seriously if she is actually his daughter. She replies that she wishes he would stop being so moody and be his old self. Lear admits that he is not his old self – he would never have accepted such disrespect in the past. He pretends not to know Goneril, and she says this is just further proof that he is losing touch with reality. Lear explodes at her and calls her a bastard, that she is no longer his daughter.

Goneril's husband, Albany, enters and Lear turns on him. Albany tells him to calm down but Lear calls for his horses, ready to leave. He tells them how foolish he was to doubt Cordelia, now that he knows what Goneril is actually like. He orders his servants to help him get ready to go. Kent and the others leave.

Albany protests that he doesn't know why Lear is so upset. The king puts a curse on Goneril that she won't bear children. He laments that how difficult it is to have an ungrateful child and rushes away, very upset, returning once to further lambast Goneril and Albany.

After Lear leaves Albany protests to Goneril, but she does not let him have his say. She calls for Oswald and orders the Fool to go to his master, the king. She tells Albany that her father has been allowed to keep a hundred knights; fifty have been let go. Oswald tells her he has written a letter to her sister and she orders him to take it to her.

Act One, Scene 5

In a room in the Duke of Albany's palace, Lear, Kent and the Fool enter. Lear tells Kent to take a letter to the Earl of Gloucester and to tell his daughter only what he needs to in response to questions about the letter. Kent promises to go straight there without stopping.

The Fool tells Lear that his daughter Regan will treat him the same as Goneril did. Then he tries to amuse the king with riddles and also tells him that he shouldn't have gotten old before he acquired some sense. Lear replies by saying he hopes he won't go mad.

Lear and the Fool leave for Gloucester's once the horses are ready.

Act Two

Act Two, Scene 1

The scene begins at the Earl of Gloucester's castle. Edmund enters and is met by a courier named Curan who informs him that he has been with his father who wants Edmund to know that Lear's daughter Regan and her husband, the Duke of Cornwall will be arriving at the castle that night. Edmund wonders what this is all about, and Curan says there are rumors going around about an impending war between the Duke of Cornwall and the Duke of Albany.

After Curan leaves Edmund expresses to himself how happy that his father will be coming there late that night as it falls in with his scheme to turn Gloucester against Edgar, his legitimate son. Just then, Edgar appears. In an aside to the audience, Edmund says that he knows his father is hiding, listening to his two sons.

Edmund tells Edgar to run away, using a dramatic whispering voice and pretending to be frightened for his brother. He intimates that Edgar has been speaking against the Duke of Cornwall, who is coming to the castle. If he leaves at night, he will be able to escape.

Edgar denies that he has said anything against Cornwall. Edmund tells him their father is coming and suggests to Edgar that they should pretend to engage in swordfight. Edgar is confused but does as Edmund says. Edmund brandishes his sword and calls out for Edgar to surrender, and then tells him, in a whisper, to run, which the young man does. Edmund cuts his arm slightly and calls for his father.

Gloucester arrives and asks where Edgar went and sends servants in pursuit of him. Edmund tells his father that Edgar has turned against Gloucester, supporting Albany. Gloucester orders that Edgar be killed if he is found. He intends to block the seaports so his son cannot leave the country.

Suddenly trumpets are heard, announcing the Duke of Cornwall's arrival. Cornwall has already heard about Edgar's supposed treachery and commiserates with Gloucester. Regan says she remembers him as one of her father's knights, and Edgar, in fact, is Lear's godson. Gloucester claims that some of the knights have turned against Lear, and have influenced Edgar.

Cornwall turns to Edmund and commends him for being a good son to Gloucester. The Earl tells them how Edmund revealed the treasonous plot and the young man promises to serve Cornwall.

Regan tells Gloucester they are there to seek his advice about "differences" that relate to her father and her sister Goneril – they want Gloucester's advice.

Act Two, Scene 2

It is almost dawn the next morning. Kent and Oswald are together outside Gloucester's castle. Oswald asks Kent if he is a servant there and where they can put their horses. Kent tells him he can park them in the mud and Oswald retorts in a bold way. Kent tells him he knows Oswald is a knave and a rascal, and hurls more than a dozen insults at him.

Oswald mildly replies that he can't imagine why someone who doesn't even know him could be so insulting. Kent reminds him about tripping him two days before, right in front of the king. He challenges Oswald to a swordfight, accusing of him of plotting against the king, with his mistress Goneril. He goads Oswald further, again challenging him to fight. Oswald merely calls for help while Kent continues to insult him and hits him with his sword.

Edmund enters with his rapier drawn. He orders them to break it up and Kent challenges him, as well. Cornwell enters with Regan, Gloucester, and a brace of servants. Gloucester demands to know what is going on. Regan identifies them as messengers of her father and of her sister.

Oswald begins to explain what's going on by first insulting Kent's more advanced years. Kent again goes into a rant of insults and the Duke of Cornwall steps in, telling Kent to be quiet, to show some respect. Kent roars that he has no respect for the likes of Oswald, who has no ethics, who does merely as his mistress or master tells him. By the end of his rant, he insults Cornwall, challenging him to a fight. Cornwall asks him if he has lost his mind.

Gloucester wants a further explanation and Kent merely says that no man could hate another as he and Oswald do. He tells Cornwall that he just doesn't like the look of Oswald. Cornwall tells him that undoubtedly he has been praised for being straightforward in the past, but now he is being merely insulting, that honesty is not about being rude. He wonders if that behind Kent's bluntness there is a crafty scheming mind.

Kent mocks this theory but calms down enough to explain that Oswald is not to be trusted. Cornwall wants Oswald to explain what he did to set Kent off. Oswald claims he didn't do anything that the king struck him by mistake, and Kent assumed he was guilty of something and tripped him, mostly just to impress the king. Kent scoffs at this, calling him a coward. Cornwall threatens to put Kent in the stocks, but Kent says he is too old to learn from being in the stocks and his honorable purpose is to serve the King. If they put him in the stocks, they insult the King. Cornwall insists on sending for the stocks and Regan backs him up.

The stocks are brought in; Gloucester pleads with Cornwall not to do this, but the Duke says he will take all responsibility. Regan says it is only right that her sister's servant be avenged. They put Kent in the stocks and leave him. Gloucester apologizes for Cornwall's conduct and leaves.

When they leave Kent pulls out a letter to read: it is from Cordelia. Then he sleeps.

Act Two, Scene 3

Edgar, Gloucester's legitimate son, is in the woods. He says that he has heard himself described as an outlaw. He had hidden in the hollow trunk of a tree and was not found. He knows he can't escape by sea as the ports are being watched. He announces that he is going disguises himself as the poorest man alive; he will wear filthy clothes and beg for money.

Act Two, Scene 4

The Earl of Kent, still in disguise, is in the stocks at Gloucester's castle. King Lear enters with his Fool. Lear is saying he is worried about his messenger (Kent) not being sent back to him.

Lear spots Kent in the stocks and the Fool jeers at him. Lear demands to know why Kent is being punished. Kent replies that it was his daughter and son-on-law who are responsible. Lear does not believe that they would do this, and they argue about it. Lear says that it is an outrage to treat the King's officer in such a way. Kent explains he tried to deliver the King's messages but that he had been interrupted by Goneril's Oswald so he threatened him with his word. When Goneril and Albany showed up, they insisted Kent be put in the stocks.

Fool sings a song about children who curry favor with their rich fathers and Lear laments how his children are breaking his heart. Kent tells him Goneril is inside and Lear rushes off.

Kent asks why there are so few men in the King's entourage and the Fool says people always desert a lost cause. As he puts it, if you hang on to a big wheel as it goes downhill, you are bound to be hurt – but hanging on to it as it goes up gives you a free ride. Kent asks him where the Fool learns his wise sayings, and the Fool answers "not in the stocks, fool".

Lear returns with Gloucester, complaining that Goneril and her husband won't speak to him: they are full of excuses. Gloucester says Albany is obstinate and always wants his own way. Lear impatiently says he wants to speak to Cornwall and his wife, Lear's other daughter Regan (he is resentful that he has to keep asking for an audience with his own daughter). He looks at Kent and loses his temper, demanding to know why his servant is in the stocks, where a king's servant should never be.

The Duke of Cornwall enters, with Regan and a few servants. Lear and Cornwall greet each other, and Regan says she is happy to see her father. Kent is let out of the stocks, and Lear tells him before he leaves that he will speak to him later.

Lear turns to Regan and tells her that Goneril is wicked. Regan tells him he is being too critical of her sister; Goneril would never let their father down. Lear disagrees and Regan tells him that he is getting old, and he should realize that there others who can govern better now. She asks him to forgive Goneril.

Lear mocks Regan by getting down on his knees and pretending to beg forgiveness from Goneril, to excuse him from his foolishness as he is old. Regan scoffs at him and tells him to return to Goneril but he refuses. He wishes the vengeance of heaven on her and her unborn children and utters all sorts of curses upon her head.

Regan questions her father's loyalty to *her* and Lear says he will never curse her for she is a good daughter. Lear then asks who put Kent in the stocks but at the same time a trumpet sounds, announcing Goneril's arrival. The sisters embrace. Cornwall admits to Lear that he put Kent in the stocks. Regan tells her father to stop fussing, that if he dismisses half his men, and stays with Goneril until the end of his allotted month, he can then come to her.

Lear refuses to dismiss his men, saying he'd rather live rough, rather swear his loyalty to Cordelia's husband, the King of France. Regan wonders why he can't be happy with fifty followers; that any more than that make it difficult for whomever he is staying with. Goneril wonders why he needs any men at all, when there are so many in his daughters' households. Lear protests that he needs these men, that without them he is nothing. He rants for a while and then leaves with Gloucester, the Fool and a Gentleman. Regan mutters that their small house cannot cope with her father's retinue. She is willing to house him, but not his followers; Goneril agrees with her.

Gloucester returns and tells them Lear is in a rage and is leaving, but he doesn't know where. He is worried about weather and road conditions outside but Goneril, Regan and Cornwall dismiss his worries, saying Lear is a grown man and knows what he is doing.

Act Three

Act Three, Scene 1

Out on the heath, a storm is raging. Kent meets a Gentleman there and recognizes him as one of Lear's followers; he asks him where the King is. He replies that Lear has left in a rage, into the storm, in desperation at what he views as a betrayal. He is alone except for his Fool, who is trying to keep his spirits up.

Kent tells the Gentleman that things are not rosy between Cornwall and Albany and that they have servants who are willing to talk, to betray them by supplying the King of France with inside information about the kingdom. In fact, Kent says, there is an army from France in the kingdom as they speak. The Gentleman wants to know more detail, but Kent refuses to tell him more, but gives him a ring to give to Cordelia – she will know who it is from.

Kent will say no more and suggests they go their separate ways and look for the King and to shout if one of them finds him.

Act Three, Scene 2

On another part of the heath, Lear and the Fool appear. Lear lifts his hands to the skies and exhorts the winds to blow, and the clouds to drench them with rain. The Fool complains that he'd rather be dry. Lear shouts that he can trust the elements; they are what they are, not ungrateful and unkind like his daughters. The Fool protests that a smart man with brains would find a house to store his head and hat. The Fool sings a song that hints he thinks the King is putting his vanity before common sense.

Suddenly Kent arrives. The Fool answers that there is a wise man and a Fool. Kent asks if the King is there, exclaiming that the men are out on such a night. Lear says it is the gods creating the tempest, to weed out their enemies. He shouts that he is more sinned against that sinning.

Kent notices Lear has removed his hat and begs him to find shelter, that there is a place not far away where he can rest while Kent goes back to Lear's daughters and convince them to make peace with their father. Lear agrees to go the shelter, draping his arm around the Fool, saying he feels sorry for him. Fool sings another little ditty about how Lear must make the best of a bad situation.

Kent and Lear head to the shelter and the Fool recites another poem, attributed to Merlin the magician, who the Fool says will be born in the future.

Act Three, Scene 3

The scene opens in a room in Gloucester's castle. It is dark. Gloucester and Edmund appear, with lit torches.

Gloucester is grumbling to Edmund about Goneril and Regan and their husbands – how they have taken over his house, and order him about, particularly concerning Lear. They will not allow him to stick up for the King. Edmund agrees that this is outrageous. Gloucester tells him that Duke Cornwall and Duke Albany, have had a serious disagreement and Gloucester himself has received a letter about it. France's army has landed, and he must take Lear's side, but does not want the Dukes to know this. He warns Edmund to be careful and leaves. Edmund sees this as a chance to usurp his father and seize power – he goes to tell Cornwall what his father has told him in confidence.

Act Three, Scene 4

On the heath, at the shelter door, Lear enters with Kent and the Fool. Kent welcomes him in, telling him the night is too wild for any creature to endure. Lear tells him to leave him in peace, that he hardly notices the storm when his heart is broken so. The treachery of his daughters is tearing him apart. Kent urges him to go into the shelter and Lear suggests he go in himself, if he needs a break from the storm. Lear also convinces the Fool to enter and says he is going to pray first.

Suddenly the Fool rushes out – he has heard Edgar's voice. Kent demand that the young man show himself. Edgar appears, disguised as a madman. He behaves bizarrely, ordering Lear and the other men away. He refers to himself as Tom and says he is hounded, chased, and is now freezing cold. He pretends to fight an imaginary pursuer.

Lear begins to rage against his daughters and Edgar responds by spouting a nonsense rhyme. The Fool says the storm is making everyone crazy. Lear demands to know who "Tom" truly is, and Edgar makes up a story about being a Don Juan, a promiscuous lover, and that caused his downfall. Lear takes pity on him, and begins to take off his clothes to give to Edgar who is almost naked. The Fool talks him out of it, and Gloucester approaches with a torch, and the Fool says he will make them a fire. Edgar claims Gloucester is an evil fiend, a bogey-man who walks at night.

Gloucester asks Kent how the King is and Lear demands to know who he actually is. Edgar continues with his incoherent ramblings. Gloucester shakes his head over this lunatic, this "Tom".

Gloucester says he is there to support Lear, against the wishes of Goneril, Regan, and the Dukes. He wants the King to come to his house. Lear begins to speak to Edgar, and Kent tells Gloucester he fears the master's mind is failing. Gloucester says it is no wonder he is losing is mind, with his daughters' betrayal – he himself has been betrayed by his own son and knows how it feels.

Lear herds them all into the shelter, his arm around "Tom", who he calls his "philosopher". Kent whispers to Gloucester to humor the King, and they all go into the shelter.

Act Three, Scene 5

Back in a room in Gloucester's castle, Cornwall enters with Edmund. Cornwall has a letter in his hand, which he waves excitedly, calling for his revenge. Edmund hypocritically expresses his regret of honoring his loyalty to Cornwall ahead of his love for his father. Cornwall reassures him that it was his brother Edgar's evil nature that is the cause of Edmund's dilemma. Edmund says that he wonders why loyalty to his country makes him feel so guilty.

Edmund tells Cornwall that the letter is holding is proof of Edgar's treachery. He tells him to come with him to see his wife, the Duchess Regan. Then he wants him to find his father Gloucester so he can be arrested. Edmund agrees to remain loyal to Cornwall, and the Duke replies he will become Edmund's new father and a more loving one.

Act Three, Scene 6

Gloucester and Kent enter a farmhouse room near the castle. Gloucester states that this is a much better place for the King than the rough shelter. He goes off to find some supplies. Kent thanks him for his kindness, saying Lear has lost his mind and needs help.

Lear comes in, with Edgar ("Tom") and the Fool. Edgar is talking nonsense. Lear is muttering about his ungrateful daughters, calling them she-foxes. The Fool is making philosophical statements, but no one seems to be listening to him. Edgar begins to sing, and the Fool joins in.

Kent invites Lear to lie down and rest, but the King says he wants to see his daughters on trial first. He tells Edgar to take his place as a judge and Kent is one of the magistrates. Edgar begins to sing nursery rhymes. Lear points to an empty seat and pretends that Goneril is sitting there – he tells Edgar and Kent that she must be tried for kicking her father, the King. Suddenly he stands up and waves his arm, saying they have let her escape. Kent begs him to take control of himself.

Edgar says to himself that he is tears of sympathy for Lear and going to ruin his disguise. Meanwhile, Lear claims the little household dogs are barking at him. Edgar says he will drive them away and sings a song about ridding them of the "curs".

Lear wishes the dogs on his daughter Regan. Kent again tries to soothe him, but the King continues to talk nonsense.

Gloucester comes in and asks for the King. Kent tells him his mind
has totally broken down. Gloucester urges him to get Lear on a
stretcher and escape from the area, to take him to Dover where they
will be protected. He says they are to follow him, and he will show
them the way and give them some provisions.

Kent and the Fool carry Lear away, with Gloucester helping.

Edgar tells the audience after they are gone that his own miseries
don't seem so bad now that he has seen the King in such a state, in
the worst kind of suffering, which is in the mind. He hopes Lear
makes a safe escape.

Act Three, Scene 7

The Duke of Cornwall, Goneril, and Regan, Edmund, and a group of servants enter a room in Gloucester's castle. Cornwall tells Goneril to find a messenger to send to her husband Albany; Cornwall wants his brother-in-law to see the letter Edmund showed him. He announces that the French army has landed and that the traitor Gloucester must be found. Goneril and Regan agree Gloucester must be executed. Cornwall says he will take care of Gloucester and tells Goneril that her husband must be warned so they can prepare for war. He says his farewells and tells Edmund to stay behind.

Oswald, Goneril's servant, enters, saying the King has been taken away by Gloucester, who has been spotted with some of his men heading for Dover. The men leave to pursue Gloucester, and it is not long before he is captured and brought in, held tightly by Cornwall's men. Gloucester is outraged that his guests are holding him prisoner. Cornwall tells his men to tie him up. Regan spits out that he is a traitor, which he denies and she responds by pulling his beard.

Cornwall accuses Gloucester of conspiring with the French, that they have proof. They demand to know where he has sent the King, and he tells them Dover, and they demand to know why. He tells them he took pity on Lear, in his madness, caused by his daughters' treachery, and he decided to send him somewhere safe. Cornwall is so angry he threatens to kick Gloucester and makes good his threat, stomping on the man's eyes.

One of Cornwall's servants admonishes him to stop. Regan turns on the servant and angrily calls him a dog. The servant says if she were a man, he would fight her. He and Cornwall begin to fight. Regan runs a sword through the servant who spoke against her, killing him.

Gloucester loses both his eyes in the melee and complains of darkness, asking to see his son Edmund. Regan tells him that is Edmund who betrayed him, it was he who told them the "truth". Gloucester now knows that his legitimate son, Edgar, was wronged. Regan orders Gloucester thrown out of his own castle and a servant pushes the blinded man out.

Cornwall complains to Regan that he has been hurt, that he is bleeding badly. They leave. Afterwards, the servants speak among themselves, disgusted with how things are turning out. They leave to help Gloucester.

Act Four

Act Four, Scene 1

Edgar is on the heath, saying it is better to be openly despised than to be flattered by others who secretly despise you. Life must be enjoyed when it is at its best, and one must know that when things are at their worst, they can only get better. He welcomes the wind that swirls around him and the other natural elements.

Gloucester approaches him, with an Old Man. Edgar is astonished to see his father led by a commoner. The Old Man is saying how he has been a Gloucester tenant for eighty years, and he wishes to help his master. Gloucester beseeches him to be gone, that his help might be more of a hindrance. The Old Man reminds him that he cannot see, but Gloucester says he has nowhere to go, that all he wants to do is be near his son Edgar once again.

"Tom" speaks, and Gloucester identifies his voice as the miserable beggar he met earlier. Edgar asks what has happened to Gloucester's eyes. Gloucester tells the Old Man to go on ahead and get some clothes for the beggar, and they will meet up with him on the way to Dover. The Old Man protests, saying the beggar is mad, but Gloucester insists he go and bring clothes to them later.

Edgar whispers to the audience that he cannot keep up this charade. Gloucester asks "Tom" if he knows the way to Dover. Tom answers in gibberish and Gloucester offers him some money, asking again if he knows how to reach Dover. Tom relents and saying yes, gives him his arm.

Act Four, Scene 2

Goneril and Edmund are near the Duke of Albany's palace, having travelled from Gloucester's palace together. Oswald enters. Goneril asks him where his master (Albany) is. Oswald says he is inside, but is acting rather strangely, maintaining that Gloucester is not the enemy but that Edmund is the one to be feared.

Goneril turns to Edmund and tells him as her husband is "cowardly" and won't take any action against the young man, he should leave quickly and return to the Duke of Cornwall, and lead his army against Gloucester. Goneril hints at the murder of Albany; that Edmund will commit, at "a mistress's command", meaning herself. She says she must take up the role of the man of the household. She kisses Edmund, and he pledges his loyalty to her. After she leaves she complains about having to share her bed with a fool (Albany).

Albany enters, and Goneril snidely remarks that he finally decided to look for her. Her husband tells her he doesn't trust her, and thinks her treatment of her father is unnatural. Goneril scoffs at his comments. Albany tells her that evil people only understand evil actions, they cannot understand goodness. He also puts the blame on his brother-in-law, the Duke of Cornwall. Goneril calls him a fool and tells him no-one can be trusted. Albany counters with saying if he let his emotions rule, he would kill her. Goneril makes fun of him, saying he is not particularly manly.

A messenger arrives and tells them that Cornwall is dead from an injury inflicted by his servant while the Duke was attacking Gloucester, taking out his eye. The messenger tells them that Gloucester lost his second eye, as well. The messenger asks them to quickly answer the letter he has brought with him. Goneril takes it, saying she will read it and answer it. The messenger tells Albany that he met Edmund going back to Gloucester's palace. Albany expresses his loyalty and gratitude to the blinded Gloucester.

Act Four, Scene 3

The French army is encamped at Dover, and Kent enters with a Gentleman. The French king has returned to his own kingdom to attend to an urgent matter and has left the French Marshal, La Far, in charge. Kent asks the Gentleman if the Queen of France, Lear's third daughter Cordelia, was upset when she heard news of her father. He said she shed some tears but kept her emotions under control, like a true queen. She did rail against her sisters, finding their behavior unbelievable. Kent comments on how strange it is that the same parents can have children that are so different.

Kent informs him that Lear is in Dover, but his lucid moments are few and far between. He does not want to see Cordelia, mainly because of his own embarrassment of how he treated her before she married the King of France. The Gentleman tells Kent that the armies of Albany and Cornwall are on the march, ready to take on anyone threatening their power. Kent hints that he won't forget the Gentleman's help when he reveals his true identity.

Act Four, Scene 4

At a different location at the French camp near Dover, Cordelia enters with a doctor, talking about her father and his madness. He has been found wearing a crown of wild-growing plants and singing loudly. The doctor says that a good sleep will do Lear the world of good to restore his senses; the King has had so little sleep it is no wonder his mind is wandering.

A messenger arrives and tells them the British army is approaching, and Cordelia replies that they are ready. She adds that they are not at war due to ambition, but due to love for her father.

Act Four, Scene 5

Regan enters a room in Gloucester's castle. Behind her is her faithful Oswald, who is carrying a letter. Regan asks him if her brother-in-law's army has set out, and he replies yes, but mostly under the guidance of Goneril, who is the better soldier than Albany. She also wants to know what was in Goneril's letter to Edmund, but Oswald says he does not know. Regan comments that Edmund has gone off on a "serious matter" and hints that it is to kill Gloucester by saying it was foolish to let the man live after he was blinded.

Oswald says he must take the letter and go after Edmund, but Regan urges him to wait until the troops leave the following day. Oswald does not think that is a good idea; he should leave immediately. Regan petulantly says she doesn't understand why he has to deliver it by hand, why couldn't someone else just find Edmund and tell him what Goneril has to say. Regan says she suspects Goneril's feelings for Edmund are the feelings that should be directed at her husband Albany; she further says she has reached an "agreement" with Edmund herself, now that Cornwall is dead. She instructs Oswald to tell Goneril this and advise her to use her common sense when she responds. Regan sends him on his way and says there is a reward for anyone who ends Gloucester's life.

Act Four, Scene 6

Near Dover Gloucester enters, led by Edgar, who is now dressed like a rustic peasant. Gloucester, not able to see, asks Edgar when they will reach the top of the hill and the young man assures him that they are climbing it, and will get there soon. Gloucester argues that the ground seems level and Edgar scoffs at this, asking him if he can't hear the sea, which is close by. Gloucester says he can't and Edgar half-jokes that his other senses must be fading, as well. The Earl agrees it is possible, but says he has noticed Edgar's speech is more refined than it was before.

Edgar stops and pretends he is at the edge of the cliff, although he is actually in the middle of a field. He exclaims at how scary it is to look over the edge, and how it makes him dizzy. The birds he can see flying over the sea look as small as insects. He can see a man below on the beach, who looks like a mere dot, and the fishermen look like mice. He describes the visual scene to Gloucester and comments that the sound of the sea cannot be heard from so high up.

Gloucester asks to be led to the edge of the cliff and Edgar obliges. Gloucester gives him a purse with a jewel in it, to reward him for helping the Earl. Edgar pretends to leave. Gloucester falls on his knees and begins to pray to the gods, renouncing the world, and ends with a blessing on Edgar, his missing son, if he is still alive. He turns in Edgar's direction and says a final farewell. He throws himself forward, as though he is on the edge of the cliff.

Edgar calls to Gloucester, asking him if he is alive and of course, the Earl is simply lying on the ground. Edgar exclaims that it is a miracle he is still alive, after falling such a distance. He begs Gloucester to speak. He tells him to look up and see the chalky cliff.

60

Gloucester reminds Edgar that he cannot see. He is distraught that he was unable to kill himself. Edgar helps him stand up and asks him how he is. He then tells him the gods have decided to let him live.

Suddenly Lear appears, dressed in wild flowers. He appears to have utterly lost his mind, and Edgar comments on this. Lear announces that he, and only he, is the King. He moves from one subject to another, gesturing and speaking as though he has a partner in conversation. He asks Edgar for the password, and lets Edgar "pass" – at this point Gloucester says he knows his voice and asks him if he isn't the King. Lear says he is and then goes into a rant about sexual behavior, that below the belt everything is controlled by the devil and everything in hell as well.

Gloucester begs to pay homage to Lear by kissing his hand. Lear reacts suspiciously to the Earl's damaged blind eyes. He tries to get Gloucester to read something, but, of course, he cannot, and Lear shows him no pity, saying one does not need eyes to know the ways of the world. Fine robes and symbols of office only hide sin, not eradicate it – but the poor are always prosecuted first and most harshly. Lear begins to babble again, and Edgar remarks that sanity and insanity exist side by side.

Lear tells the Earl he knows who he is – Gloucester. He begins to give Gloucester a good speech but soon is off on a tangent, threatening to kill his sons-in-law.

A Gentleman and Attendants arrive, looking for the King. Lear thinks he is being taken prisoner in war and says they will be able to collect a ransom for him. He also asks for a doctor, for he is "cut to the brains". The Gentleman tells him he can have whatever he wants, that his loving daughter Cordelia has sent them to find him.

Edgar speaks to the Gentleman, asking him if there is an impending battle. He replies that only someone who is deaf doesn't know about it, and the other army is closing in on them, expected to arrive by the hour. The Gentleman leaves.

Edgar addresses Gloucester as "father", and the Earl demands to know who he is. He replies that he is a broken man, and offers his father his hand. Gloucester blesses him.

Oswald enters and calls out to the Earl that he is a man with a price on his head and is a miserable old traitor. He pulls out his sword, as though to kill Gloucester. Edgar steps forward to protect his father and Oswald threatens to kill him as well if he does not get out of the way. Edgar asks Oswald to just let them, a pair of poor peasant folk, move on. Oswald again threatens him, and the two of them fight, Edgar knocking Goneril's servant down. Oswald, thinking he is dying, offers Edgar his purse and to bury his body properly. He asks him to give the letters he is carrying to Edmund, the Earl of Gloucester. Edgar recognizes him as Goneril's servant. Oswald dies.

The letter Edgar rips open reveals Goneril's plot to have Edmund, who she desires, to kill her husband. Edgar decides to hold on to the letter to show Albany how treacherous his wife actually is.

The sound of drums is heard. Edgar tells his father to come with him, and he will lead them to safety.

Act Four, Scene 7

Cordelia, Kent, a doctor and a Gentleman enter a tent in the French army's camp. Cordelia is expressing her gratitude to Kent. Kent says it is nothing, just the truth, which deserves no reward. Cordelia wants him to change his clothes back to those suiting his status, but he says no, he wants to remain anonymous for a while.

Cordelia asks the doctor how her father is; she is worried about his fractured mind. The Doctor suggests they wake him and see how he is doing. Soon Lear is brought in, carried on a chair, still asleep. He has been cleaned up and wearing new clothes. Cordelia beseeches that he wake up and be normal again. She kisses his forehead and strokes his hair, lamenting the terrible experiences he's been through. Lear awakens and says he is in hell. He does not recognize Cordelia. Slowly he becomes more lucid but is still confused. He is not sure he knows his daughter, and kneels at her feet, saying he does not recognize where they are, or the clothes he is wearing. Then he addresses her as Cordelia, and asks her not to weep for him. He says she does not love him, and her sisters have wronged him.

Kent tells Lear he is in his own kingdom, which the King does not believe. The Doctor warns them that they must go slowly so he can recover his wits. The King leaves with his daughter, the Doctor, and their Attendants. Kent tells the Gentleman that remains behind that Edmund, Gloucester's bastard son, has taken command of Cornwall's people. The Gentleman replies that he has heard that Edgar is in Germany with Gloucester. The Earl dismisses these rumors and says they must get ready for battle.

Act Five

Act Five, Scene 1

Edmund, Regan, Officers and Soldiers enter the British army camp at Dover. Edmund orders one of the Officers to find out what the Duke of Albany's plan is. Regan tells Edmund that her sister's steward, Oswald, as been killed. Regan tries to find out from Edmund if he loves her sister Goneril, if they are actually lovers. Edmund denies everything, and she begs him to stay away from her sister.

Goneril enters with her husband and Soldiers. She murmurs that she would rather lose the battle than lose Edmund to her sister. Albany tells Regan and Edmund that Lear is with Cordelia, and that they do not wish to fight their father, but that they must defend themselves against the French. Goneril urges Regan to join them in the fight against their common enemy. Neither sister trusts the other alone with Edmund.

Suddenly Edgar appears, in disguise and begs Albany to let him speak. Albany tells the others to go on ahead. Edgar tells him to open the letter he has brought, and if he wins the battle to call for him. If he loses, it will make no difference. Albany asks him to stay while he reads it, but Edgar says he has been ordered not to remain there. The young man leaves, and Edmund returns. He tells Albany it is time to gather their troops for the onslaught. Their scouts have made an estimate of how many soldiers are on the other side, and what equipment they have.

Albany goes, and Edmund remains behind. He tells the audience he has promised to love both sisters and each are suspicious of the other; this suits his ambitions. He cannot have both if both remain alive, and Goneril is still married while Regan is a widow. He will leave it up to Goneril to decide how to get rid of her husband – but Edmund knows that Lear and Cordelia will never be free again if he has his way.

Act 5, Scene 2

In a field between the camps of the French and the British, Lear is seen walking with Cordelia and some of their Soldiers. Edgar appears with Gloucester and leads him to the shelter of a tree, asking him to pray for the right side to win, and to wait for him there. The young man leaves.

The sounds of war grow louder and then the sound of a retreat is heard. Edgar suddenly reappears, telling Gloucester that they must go. King Lear has lost, and he has been captured along with Cordelia. Gloucester protests, that he may as well die there under the tree. Edgar convinces him to get up and they leave.

Act 5, Scene 3

Edmund is victorious and is at the British camp at Dover. Lear and Cordelia are there as his prisoners. He orders some officers to take them away and keep a close watch over them. Lear says he and Cordelia will enjoy themselves in prison, praying, singling, and telling each other stories. He tells her not to cry, not to let their enemies make her weep.

Edmund gives an Officer a letter and tells him to follow Lear and his daughter to prison and intimates he wants them killed; there will be a monetary award for the Officer when the deed is done.

Albany, Regan, and Goneril enter. Albany asks Edmund to turn his two prisoners over to him. Edmund says he wants Lear to remain under guard, in consideration of his age until Albany puts them on trial. Cornwall takes issue with Edmund's attitude; he says the young man is acting like an equal, not like his subject. Regan intervenes and says it is up to her to decide how to rank him, and that she has marriage on her mind. Goneril sarcastically says if only Regan could get a chance at such a prize.

Regan turns to Edmund and offers herself and her holdings to him. Goneril wants to know if she will marry him. Albany rebukes his wife for speaking out of turn. Edmund turns on Albany and says he has no more power over him than his wife does and Albany swears, calling him a bastard. Regan sticks to her guns and tells Edmund that what belongs to her is his.

Albany declares that he is going to arrest Edmund and Goneril, too. He tells Regan that Goneril has been acting under the orders of Edmund and that if wants to marry the young man, she must have Albany's permission. Goneril mocks him.

Albany throws down his gauntlet and challenges Edmund to fight. Regan begins to wail piteously. Edmund enthusiastically throws his own gauntlet down, stating he is more than ready to take on Albany. The two men call for a herald to supervise the duel. Regan moans that she is ready to faint. Officers take her away.

A herald arrives and blows a trumpet, while Albany announces that on the third blow, any man who believes Edmund is a traitor should step forward. On the third trumpet blow, Edgar appears, armed. The herald asks him who he is and what he is doing there. Edgar draws his sword and challenges his half-brother Edmund. He calls him a traitor and challenges him to prove otherwise. Edmund responds that he will rise to the challenge and the two men begin to fight.

Edmund soon falls, wounded. In the background Goneril calls out to Edmund that he is being tricked – that he should never have taken up the fight with an unknown enemy. Albany sneers at her, indicating he has the letter his wife wrote to Edmund declaring her love for him; he waves it in her face, taunting her to "read thine own evil". Goneril exchanges threats with him, and then leaves, extremely upset. Albany orders one of his entourage to follow her and make sure she does no harm.

Edmund, injured, admits that he has done serious wrong, and it will soon be revealed. He begs Edgar to tell him who he is, if he is a nobleman, to forgive him. Edgar tells him that he is their father's son, and that because Gloucester fathered Edmund the traitor, he is now blind. Edmund admits his treachery.

Albany embraces Edgar and asks forgiveness if he has wronged him or his father. Edgar tells him the story of how he discovered the plot against the Earl. Edmund tells him the speech has touched him, and Albany urges Edgar to say no more, for the tale has brought him close to tears. But Edgar wants to clear the reputation of the wronged Kent and tells Albany how the man saved Gloucester and protected Lear, never giving up his loyalty to the King.

Suddenly a Gentleman enters, holding a blood stained knife and barely able to speak – he finally tells them "she's dead". He tells Albany it is his wife, Goneril, who is dead, and that she poisoned her sister Regan. Edmund speaks up that he was engaged to marry both of them, and now they will die together.

Kent appears, saying he is coming to say goodnight to his master, Lear. Attendants enter with the bodies of Regan and Goneril. Kent is surprised to see the sisters, now both dead. Albany orders their faces covered.

Edmund makes one last attempt at redeeming himself – he tells the men to get to the castle quickly, for he has ordered the deaths of Lear and Cordelia. Albany gives Edgar a reprieve, who orders one of his Officers to go and save the King and his last living daughter. Albany orders servants to carry Edmund away.

Lear arrives, carrying Cordelia, who appears dead. He is howling in misery and screams abuse at Albany. Kent moans that the end of the world has surely come. Suddenly Lear shouts that Cordelia is alive; she is still breathing. Kent is ecstatic. Lear tells him to get away, and Kent tries to explain that he is his loyal supporter. Lear moans over Cordelia and announces that he is the one who killed the man who was trying to hang the young woman. He again asks Kent who he is, and finally seems to recognize him, although confused about Kent's actions.

Lear drops suddenly, in a faint. Kent and Edgar soon realize the King is dead. Kent comments that Lear was living on borrowed time and that death is probably a blessing. Albany announces a time of mourning and tells Kent and Edgar that they will now rule the kingdom – Kent's reply indicates that he too believes his time on Earth is limited.

Edgar says the burden of ruling the kingdom must now be taken up by the young, who cannot fully appreciate how much the generation before them have suffered.

About BookCaps

We all need refreshers every now and then. Whether you are a student trying to cram for that big final, or someone just trying to understand a book more, BookCaps can help. We are a small, but growing company, and are adding titles every month.

Visit www.bookcaps.com to see more of our books, or contact us with any questions.